The Clown

Dmitry Goykhman

* * *

You are fifteen – it couldn't be much better
The world is pristine in the dew
And in this evanescent operetta
The place of diva is vacant for you

* * *

The earth has hailed one more newcomer
With no hair and mouth toothless
He is as fragile as gossamer
But there'll come his time for business

I meant to say by phrase preceding
That when he grows up to heaven
He won't be Atlas to back the buildings
But Zeus to make them happen

* * *

Where is the world going?
What is its destined path?
Will people still be bowling
In two hundred years or less?

Or will the Earth forfeit its claim
To bear fruits of effervescent life
And will become of thoughtlessness domain
Another planet-grave of which the skies are rife?

But why, one might disdainfully inquire
Why pose all these questions dire?
Who, with his mind possessed of even negligible luster,
Will ever be afraid of perishing from nuclear disaster?

Alas, there's a greater cause for consternation
And that is humankind's degeneration
When people will by robots be replaced
Then monkeys happily will add to their race

* * *

The night has shrouded my soul
The singing of the birds has ceased to set my heart astir
My life has lost its only real goal
Eternal doom will spread its wings forever more

Attracted by a woman worthy of the name of Aphrodite
To whose unearthly charms my poems vainly tried to
pay a proper due
I stand despondent, my eyes blind to the light
My only hope lying in the ocean blue

I'll rig a ship designed for distant travel
I'll carve her godly image on its bow
Let all the world behold the universe's finest marvel
And celebrate with drinks and merriment and cries of
'holy cow'.

* * *

I look at you with fiery desire
You always set my heart on fire
I touch you gently – you recoil
Oh please waste not my dreams nor spoil

Approach me and touch my hand
Oh, heart of stone, please relent
Break not my every pure dream
Oh kiss me, be my cherubim

* * *

What is a proper theme?
What's an appropriate way?
Can't one let go of a little steam
And brighten altogether boring day?

Can't one be just a bit unseemly?
Isn't decorum just a mask
With feelings shining ever so dimly?
When one plays proper one forgets one's task

* * *

Two men pull near
Two guns are drawn
One thing is clear
For death they yearn

A gun's discharge
A bullet flies
Impossible to dodge
It brings demise

One man is fallen
Another one still stands
Appears downtrodden
He cannot make amends

* * *

A baby's born
His mouth toothless
He is forlorn
He looks for nipples

A mother watches
In quiet wonder
She looks for gotchas
Can't find them yonder

A lightning flashes
The baby's crying
The mother thrashes
Protects her darling

She looks for hope
In baby's tears
His winding rope
Allays her fears

She finds redemption
In baby's shout
She made confession
She is devout

Two vases rise
Two flowers aspire
They sing demise
Of earthly choir

They sing rebirth
Of azure music
They found mirth
But not the rhyme …

* * *

I don't know what to do
I don't know what to say
Which way will fateful blow sway
And how will the cows moo?

Will milk drip down like the rain
That finishes the draught's assault
That will allay unending pain
And halo the gothic vault?

Or will it come in beastly tears
That pour down through the years
Of suffering in forests dark
Of carving life in brushes stark?

I don't know what will pass
And who will drown in morass
That drags one to its scary depth
To certain doom, to sure death

* * *

A shotgirl's dream has been fulfilled
I bought a shot for her
She beamed at me with gladness filled
And gave the shot a stir

She is in love with French cuisine
And knows Hebrew just a bit
She thinks good food is no sin
Prefers red to white meat

She likes to sing, she likes to dance
She likes to bump with hips
She brings me to a state of trance
With fullness of her lips

* * *

Who understands a woman's heart?
It is forever enigmatic
In it the subtlety of nature and sublimity of art
Combined in union pragmatic

Who ever fathoms its abysmal depth
The heights of pity and the hatred's cavern?
Who can discern in every pure breath
The gentle dove and the rapacious raven?

In every smile who sees a frown?
In every kiss the thorns of rose?
Who in her bosom cannot drown?
In her simplicity who sees a pose …?

* * *

A clown does his act
The audience laughs and cries
He spins in pirouette
And falls as in demise

The laughter does not cease
Yet tears do not flow
The laughers are at ease
Yet criers wish to know

He lies on circus floor
Sweat dripping down cheeks
He played it cool and raw
Of cadaver he reeks

He hasteth not to rise
The laughter grows quiet
The laughers paid the price
They'll break into a riot

The criers jump to feet
They stare at the clown
He played it cool and neat
But now he is down

He hasteth not to rise
His eyes are glassy blue
He paid the final price
His dream did not come true

* * *

Incite me, come
Let roses bloom
Inside me calm
I am your groom

* * *

He wants to crack my head
I don't know why
He wants me nice and dead
His humor's wry and dry

Perhaps I know why
But I won't tell you that
He wants me nice and dead
His humor's wry and dry

* * *

I remember the heat of desire
You always set my heart on fire
I think of you all night and day
You are my pleasure, you are my pain

I always want to hold you near
Please touch me gently, allay my fear
To my heart you hold the key
Oh be with me, forever be with me

Let's lock the bodies in embrace
Your heart will race, my heart will race
Together we will reach the heaven
We'll never go down, never

* * *

The time has come to make a stand
Let's doff the flimsy mask
One only to a point can pretend
Illusion cannot last

* * *

The spring is here
Its breath on my cheek
The joy is near
Come, come this week

The load's gone
My soul so light
The music's on
It feels all right

* * *

I see a glimmer in your eyes
Your smile is both strange and sympathetic
Perhaps you are a devil in disguise
Your words are both clairvoyant and prophetic

My eyes begin to follow your gaze
We now both look at heavenly expanse
I am by your angelic look amazed
But what if you will laugh at my expense?

A devil or an angel – who are you?
Disclose secretly your inner self
I don't want additional ado
I want into your nature delve

* * *

A prisoner confined,
His pose drooping
Thinks of the things refined
With his existence so gloomy

He thinks of the caresses
That he was showered with
Remembering the fallen dresses
That wiggled down in the breeze

Recalling fights and brawls
He thirsts for that elusive peace
Surrounded by filthy walls
His thirst will shortly cease

He'll find elusive peace
Ineffable as it may be
But he will always miss
That calming garden tree

* * *

The thoughts just keep on racing
They are like ships in stormy waters
There's no chance for spacing
They always are at close quarters

But finally the lull ensues
And thoughts will find repose
The gladness then will be profuse
The beauty – that of blooming rose

* * *

Release your inhibitions
Let prudish smoke dissipate
Explore completely your volitions
Completely change your fate

Enjoy the beauty of creation
Create with joy, abandon
Forget all pain and tension
Create from depths one cannot fathom

Look forward, never back
Immersed completely in the torrents
Let life be rather rack
Than full of boring moments

* * *

I don't believe in God
But a cathedral attracts me
With a strange, mystifying force
I meditate in it
It is an expression of
The forces of nature
Which drive me inexorably
In it Love, Time and Space
Are intertwined

* * *

He is an artist in the daytime
He is a criminal at night
He knows how to rhyme
He knows how to fight

His cunning is devilish
His evil deeds are dark
But he finds a certain relish
In polishing creative art

He looks you in the eyes
A devil or a saint? – you never know
Is it his beauty or his vice
That is his mystery and glow?

He is con artist par excellence
His dual nature there shines
He is a player in every romance
For him every damsel pines

* * *

To fight or not to fight?
To yield or not to yield?
The situation's very tight
Who'll be a victor on the battlefield?

Whom will the gods prefer?
Whom will the gods forget?
The answer we'll defer
Until we see the bloody end

One thing is clear, though
One man will stay alive
He will deliver finally the blow
That will resolve the scary fight

He will be without remorse
But he won't be forgiven
His battle-weary horse
Will fall as if stricken

And so the battle will end
As all the battles eventually do
A victor will stand, a loser will bend
Thus history unfurls for you

* * *

You symbolize the moon to me
You symbolize the sun, the stars, the earth
You are a mystery without which I cannot be
Without you my life becomes devoid of mirth

For me you are a blinding light
That conquers darkness's domain
Without you all world's a sheer night
You bring me pleasure, take away all pain

You are divine, you symbolize the spark
That will light up an everlasting fire
You are a savior, you bring a Noah's Ark
I feel for you unquenchable desire

You symbolize a lot of things to me
You are a melody that brightens up my day
With you I can with ease foresee
My happiness and all things gay

* * *

The sea, the mountains, the clouds
Combine idyllically in my imagination
One glance at them makes me forget my troubles
And rid my life of misery and tension

I contemplate this natural beauty
Ebullient inside, I joyfully exult
But suddenly the trumpet calls to duty
Reality returns, makes me forget all Art

The struggle between Art and Reason
Without reconciliation goes on forever
And their comrades never have committed treason
And none of warriors succumbed yet to despair

* * *

I remember when you entered my world
I remember the warmth of your body
I remember the fullness of your lips
I remember the shape of your hips

Do not leave me, now or ever
Do not let my love go spoiled
Do not look, my cherub, for another
Do not put me in eternal turmoil

* * *

Remember the good times
Let the bad times go
What's in a name? A man's soul?
Let the Spirit guide you
In uncharted waters
Let the stars beguile you
To their abodes
Let the universe sing
Its ancient melody
Raise up a drink
To conquer all maladies

* * *

Conquer all your fears
Look as always straight
No time for tears
Just accept your fate

Make the final effort
Give it all you've got
Do not respond with affront
Put over 1 the dot

Rivers will always flow
Stars will shine above
Keep your eyes aglow
The stretch might be rough

* * *

I remember the starry night
When I saw your face asudden
You appeared like a sudden light
And ennobled my being rotten

With your tender, gentle hand
You caressed my soul thirsty
No longer I felt bereft
Of all joys with life so ghostly

Your life-giving, watering touch
I'll remember as long as I be
I still love you, oh so much
Do not leave me forsaken, Thee

* * *

The time has come for masters to rebel
They've worn the heavy chains for many years
The time has come to ring the heavy bell
The time has come to put away all fears

Aristocrat of Spirit, speak the Truth
Let Truth become your sword of choice
Aristocrat of Spirit, let your Muse
Inspire you with passion as you go forth

Your Muse and Reason will unite
One giving rise to passion, one controlling it
Remain original, be never trite
And let them have a dose of your wit

* * *

Truth is a beautiful woman
and different philosophers
look at this beauty
from different perspectives,
one gazing at her naked shoulder,
another admiring the outline of her neck.
Truth, however, is a woman of infinite number of forms,
so that as long as there will be philosophers,
they will always discover
some marvelous aspect of truth to behold.

* * *

Communication line is broken
The phone's hung, the words unspoken
The train of peace has been derailed
The plan of war has been detailed

"We strive for peace!" – proclaim the bosses
While stifling every cry of slaves
"We'll help you, dear!" - and crush the roses
While their audience jumps and raves

Perhaps, they'll change and show pity
Perhaps, fatigued by nitty-gritty
They will abstain from further wreck
And will with roses frame the deck

Who is to say – you never know
But feeling is – the strife will grow
Yet hope rests – perhaps some day
The blood will stop, the peace will reign